KLASSENARBEITEN LÖSUNGEN

Englisch 6. Klasse

Hauptschule

W0270202

STARK

ISBN 978-3-86668-659-5

Lösungen

Test 1

1 4 Minuten,

Hörverstehenstext (Track 1):

London is the capital of Great Britain. A famous sight in London is Tower Bridge. The capital of France is Paris. The city is famous for its Eiffel Tower. The capital of Spain is Madrid. Spain is a country in the south-west of Europe. Hamburg is a big city in Germany but it is not the capital. The capital of Germany is Berlin. Vienna is the biggest city in Austria. It is also its capital. Rome is the capital of Italy. It is a very old city. Some buildings there are over 2 000 years old.

		right	wrong
a	The Eiffel Tower is not in London.	✓	
b	The Tower Bridge is a famous sight in Paris.		✓
c	Madrid is a country in south-western Europe.		✓
d	Hamburg is not a capital.	✓	
e	Vienna is the capital of Australia.		✓
f	Rome is a very old city.	✓	

2

2 2 Minuten,

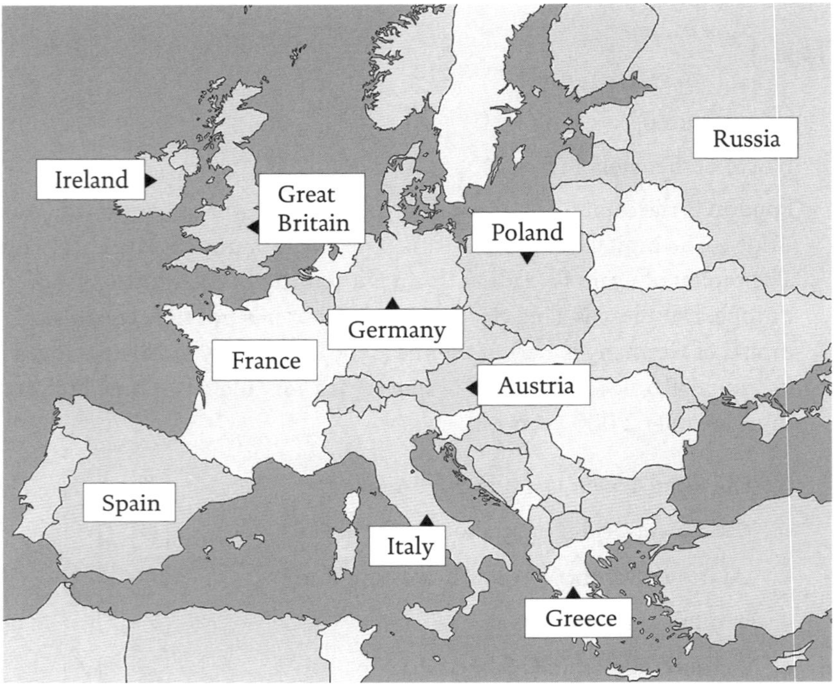

3 7 Minuten,

a I was in **Greece** with my **parents**. We went by **plane**. We stayed at a **big hotel**. We visited many **museums**. My holiday was **okay**.

b I was **in Spain** with **my family**. We went **by caravan to a campsite**. The campsite was at the **seaside**. We often went **swimming**. My holiday **was fantastic**.

c I was with my **grandmother** in **Bristol**. I often played with a **girl** called Susan. She had a **slackline** and we walked on it. My holiday was **great**.

d I stayed **at home** here in **Glasgow**. I played **with my friends**. We often played **football**. My holiday was **all right**.

4 7 Minuten,

Lösungsbeispiel:

In the summer holidays I often go to the mountains with my parents and my brother. We go hiking every day. In the evening we always play games. In the holidays I also meet my friends. Then we go swimming.

Klassenarbeit 1

1 7 Minuten,

Hörverstehenstext (Track 2):

Hi everybody. I'm Kimberley Reed. I'm a pupil at Drummond Community High School. That's a secondary school in Edinburgh. Edinburgh is in Scotland, but I'm sure you know that. I'm 13 years old and I'm in class S4. We have school uniforms. We must wear white shirts or blouses, black jumpers or cardigans, black skirts, black blazers and black shoes. Boys must wear black trousers. Jeans are not allowed.

I go to school by bus. I have to leave the house at quarter past eight. School starts at 9 o'clock. We get our lunch at school. Lessons finish at 3 o'clock, but on Fridays at 12.20. I like P.E. lessons best. I'm quite good at sports.

I also take guitar lessons at our school. I think playing an instrument is cool and the guitar is the best instrument of all. I also learn German in the language club. I know, for example, that "Goodbye" is "Auf Wiedersehen" in German.

Last year we organised a lot of activities at a home for old people in Porthaven. The old people especially liked the Scottish afternoon with tea and dancing. We also organized a "bingo afternoon". The old people really enjoyed the activities, and we hope we can continue the project next year.

a Kimberley's family **name** is Reed.
b She **goes** to school in **Edinburgh**.
c She is in **class** 4S.
d The pupils **wear** school uniforms at Drummond Community High School (DCHS).
e Kimberley has **lunch** at school.
f Her **favourite** subject is P.E.
g She **likes** to play the **guitar**.
h DCHS organized a lot of activities for **old people** in a home.
i Kimberley goes to a **language** club.

2 3 Minuten,

a Does Kimberley go to school by bike? **No, she doesn't.**
b Does she like sport lessons? **Yes, she does.**
c Does she learn French at school? **No, she doesn't.**
d Do the pupils wear jeans at school? **No, they don't.**
e Do the pupils have lunch at school? **Yes, they do.**

4 **3** 4 Minuten,

a School in Scotland starts at 9 o'clock.
b Pupils must wear school uniforms.
c The pupils have lunch at school.
d They have tests every week. / Every week they have tests.
e Lessons finish at half past three in the afternoon.
f The pupils do their homework after school.

4 4 Minuten,

a Ella is from England. She lives in London.
b Allan is from Scotland. He lives in Edinburgh.
c Vivien lives in Belfast. She is from Northern Ireland.
d Gary lives in Cardiff. He is from Wales.

5 3 Minuten,

a No, he doesn't. He goes to school by bus.
b Do Jane and Peter play football?
c Does Sarah have a laptop/computer?
d No, they don't. They have a dog.

6 9 Minuten,

Fiona fragt, ob er oft fernsieht. **Do you often watch TV?**

Ryan sagt, dass er immer am Samstag fernsieht.
I always watch TV on Saturday.

Fiona fragt, was seine Lieblingssendung *(show)* ist.
What's your favourite show?

Ryan sagt, dass er gerne *Sport live* ansieht. **I like to watch Sport live.**

Fiona fragt, wann die Sendung kommt. **When is the show?**

Ryan sagt, um 5 Uhr nachmittags. **At 5 o'clock in the afternoon.**

Ryan fragt, ob sie auch gerne Krimis *(thrillers)* sieht.
Do you like to watch thrillers, too?

Fiona verneint. **No, I don't.**

Fiona sagt, dass sie gerne Quizshows sieht. **I like to watch quiz shows.**

Test 2

1 4 Minuten,

Hörverstehenstext (Track 3):

Last Saturday I was at Alisa's birthday party. Alisa is a school friend of mine. Isabella, my best friend, was also invited. The party wasn't in Alisa's house, but in a shed in the garden. The party was from 6 o'clock till 9 o'clock in the evening. There weren't lots of children, we were only five. It was quite dark in the shed. There was no electric light. But there were some candles on the tables. The music was very loud and really cool. We all liked the songs. Only Johnny, the dog, wasn't very happy.

Last **Saturday** I was at a party.
Isabella, my best friend, **was** also invited.
The party **wasn't** in Alisa's house, but in a shed in their garden. Alisa is a school friend of mine.
The party was from 6 o'clock till 9 o'clock in the **evening**.
There **weren't** lots of children, we **were** only five.
It was quite **dark** in the shed.
There was no electric **light**.
But there were some candles on the **tables**.
The music was **very** loud and really cool.
We all liked the songs.
Only Johnny, their **dog**, wasn't very happy. He hates loud music.

2 2 Minuten,

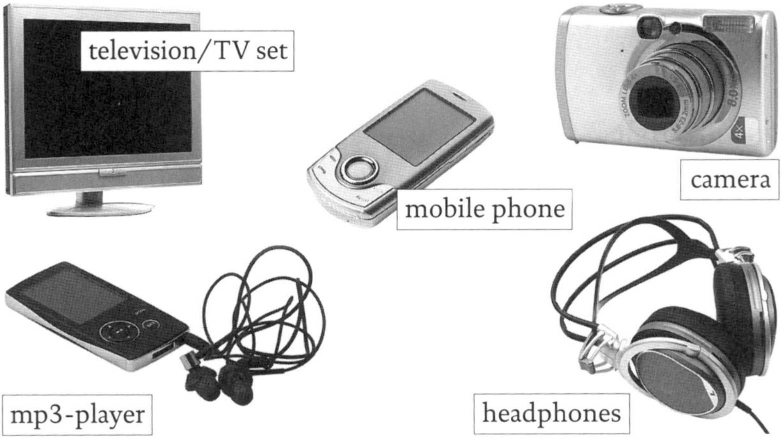

6 3 4 Minuten,

Klassenarbeit 2

1 5 Minuten,

William Shakespeare:
The most famous English writer was born in **1564**.

Isaac Newton:
The great English scientist was born in **1643**.

Lady Gaga:
The famous American singer was born in **1986**.

J. K. Rowling:
The author of the Harry Potter books was born in **1965**.

2 12 Minuten,

		city	inhabitants
1st	first	London	8 000 000
2nd	second	Glasgow	592 000
3rd	third	Edinburgh	486 000
4th	fourth	Cardiff	341 000
5th	fifth	Belfast	265 000
6th	sixth	Brighton	155 000
7th	seventh	York	135 000

3 8 Minuten,

Last week I was at the cinema with a friend.
The film wasn't good.
The title of the film was "Batman Returns".
My brother was in the football stadium.
The game/match was quite boring.

4 5 Minuten,

a You **mustn't** take photos here.
b Cyclists **can/must** ride their bikes here.
c Drivers **must** turn right.
d Drivers **must stop** here.
e Drivers **can park** here.
f Drivers **mustn't** drive faster than 30 km/h.

Test 3

1 5 Minuten,

Hörverstehenstext (Track 4):

At the electronics shop

SHOP ASSISTANT: Good morning, Madam. What can I do for you?

CUSTOMER: Good morning. I'm looking for a smartphone with a digital camera.

SHOP ASSISTANT: They are over there. Just come with me. Here they are.

CUSTOMER: How much is this blue one?

SHOP ASSISTANT: It's £ 189.99.

CUSTOMER: That's too expensive for me. Do you have anything cheaper?

SHOP ASSISTANT: Yes, wait a minute. This one is only £ 79.99. But the camera isn't as good.

CUSTOMER: That doesn't matter. I like it – but do you have it in blue?

SHOP ASSISTANT: Yes. We have it in blue, green, black and pink.

CUSTOMER: OK, I'll take a blue one.

SHOP ASSISTANT: All right. That's a nice colour.

		right	wrong
a	Die Kundin betritt das Geschäft am Vormittag.	✓	
b	Die Kundin möchte ein Smartphone ohne Kamera kaufen.		✓
c	Der Verkäufer sagt, dass das blaue Smartphone 199,99 £ kostet.		✓
d	Der Kundin sind auch 79,99 £ zu teuer für ein Smartphone.		✓
e	Die Kundin möchte ein Smartphone in rosa.		✓
f	Das Smartphone für 79,99 £ gibt es auch in rosa.	✓	
g	Die Kundin geht ohne Smartphone.		✓

2 2 Minuten,

happy	sad	angry (grumpy)	grumpy (angry)	tired	crazy

3 3 Minuten,

simple present	simple past	Grundform (deutsch)
1 we find	we *found*	*finden*
2 I m**eet**	I **met**	*treffen*
3 they **think**	they **thought**	*denken*
4 he h**as**	he **had**	*haben*
5 you **take**	you **took**	*nehmen*
6 she **tells**	she **told**	*erzählen, sagen*
7 he **is**	he w**as**	*sein*
8 she w**rites**	she **wrote**	*schreiben*

4 5 Minuten,

- a I had a birthday party last Friday. / Last Friday I had a birthday party.
- b I wore my red and white dress.
- c My father did some magic tricks.
- d That was very exciting.
- e I got a lot of presents from my family.
- f My older sister made a birthday cake with candles for me.
- g The grilled sausages were very good.

Klassenarbeit 3

1 7 Minuten,

Hörverstehenstext (Track 5):

MOTHER: Hi, Charlie.
CHARLIE: Hi, Mum.
MOTHER: How was school today? What did you learn?
CHARLIE: We learnt something about the first locomotives.
MOTHER: Oh, that sounds interesting. Where was the first steam locomotive built?
CHARLIE: In England, of course. The most famous early locomotive was called "Rocket". It was built by George and Robert Stephenson for the railway between Manchester and Liverpool. It had won a railway com-

petition at Rainhill in October 1829.

MOTHER: How fast was it?

CHARLIE: It ran at an average of 19 km/h, but its top speed was 48 km/h.

MOTHER: And when was the Manchester and Liverpool railway opened?

CHARLIE: One year after the competition, on September 15th, 1830. The locomotive was driven by a man called Joseph Locke.

MOTHER: Didn't they have railways in Germany before that?

CHARLIE: No. The first train in Germany ran between Nuremberg and Fürth in 1835. The name of the locomotive was "Adler".

MOTHER: Oh, "Adler", that's funny. "Adler" means "eagle" in English. Was it as fast as an eagle?

CHARLIE: Well, not quite. Its top speed was 65 km/h. But it ran only 48 km/h when it pulled its nine coaches. By the way, the Adler was built by the Stephensons, too. Its first driver was William Wilson. He came along with the Adler from England.

MOTHER: Wow, you're quite the expert on steam locomotives. But now sit down and enjoy your meal before it gets cold.

- a The first steam locomotive was built in *England / Germany/ Ireland.*
- b The most famous early locomotive in England was called *"Racket" / "Rocket" / "Adler".*
- c It won a locomotive competition *in Liverpool / in Rainhill / in Manchester.*
- d Its top speed was *48 km/h / 84 km/h / 65 km/h.*
- e The first locomotive in Germany ran in *1835/ 1853 / 1830.*
- f The driver of the Adler was *William Wilson / Joseph Locke / Robert Stephenson.*
- g The Adler was built in *England / Germany / Nuremberg.*

2 6 Minuten,

- a What animal do the Shorts have?
  a cat
- b Where were the Shorts on that Saturday afternoon?
  at the supermarket
- c On which floor is the Shorts' flat?
  on the first floor
- d Who saw the open balcony door first?
  Mrs Short

e Was Koshka on the balcony?
No, she wasn't.

f Where was Koshka when they saw her?
on the playground / in the sandpit

g What had she hurt?
her leg

h What do the Shorts do now whenever they go away?
(They) close the balcony door.

3 5 Minuten,

"I **looked** out of the window. I **saw** the door of the balcony open and Koshka **came** out. First she **played** with a peg *(Wäscheklammer)*. Then she **jumped** on the railing *(Geländer)* of the balcony. First she **went** along the railing. Then she **was** at the corner of the balcony railing. She **watched** the birds at the playground. I **called**: "Koshka, go down the railing!", but she didn't listen. Then I had to go and take my grandson Bob to his music lesson."

4 4 Minuten,

a He stayed in bed.
b He didn't go to school.
c He phoned a friend.
d He didn't visit his grandma.
e He watched TV.
f He had some biscuits.
g He drank a lot of tea.
h He didn't speak very much.

5 4 Minuten,

a He mustn't watch TV. He must do his homework first.
b He must clean his shoes because they are very dirty.
c He must take the dog for a walk.
d He mustn't visit his friend. He must clean his room first.
e He mustn't play computer games all day.
f He must open the bathroom window.

6 4 Minuten,

a Timmy, you **shouldn't** eat too many sweets!
b Timmy: I didn't eat **any** sweets last week.
c **Could** you open the window, please? It's so hot in here!
d Waiter: "Would you like **anything** else?"
e Guest: "I would like **something** to drink."
f Waiter: "I could offer you **some** delicious red wine."

Test 4

1 7 Minuten,

Hörverstehenstext (Track 6):

Dialogue 1

MAN: Excuse me, please. Can you tell me where I can get some stamps?

WOMAN: Oh, I'm afraid you'll have to go to the post office. Go to the end of this street and turn left. The post office is on your right.

MAN: Thank you very much!

Dialogue 2

MAN: Excuse me, sir. Can you tell me where the next public toilet is?

POLICEMAN: A toilet … You need to go to the railway station. There's one there.

MAN: Where is it?

POLICEMAN: Go straight ahead and turn left at the second crossing. The station is right ahead of you. The toilet is next to the station.

MAN: Is it far?

POLICEMAN: No, only about 200 m.

Dialogue 3

GIRL: Excuse me, please. I'd like to visit my friend in hospital, but I've lost my way. Do you know where the hospital is?

WOMAN: Yes, of course. I'm a nurse there. The best is to turn right here and then left at the next crossing. Go down the street. The hospital is in front of you at the next crossing.

GIRL: Thanks a lot.

Dialogue 4

MAN: Excuse me, please. I'm looking for the tourist office. Is it far from here?

WOMAN: No, not at all. It's just round the corner.

MAN: Sorry, I didn't understand. Where is it, you said?
WOMAN: Round the corner. Turn right at the next crossing. You'll find the tourist office on your right. There's a big "**i**" above the door.
MAN: Thank you very much.

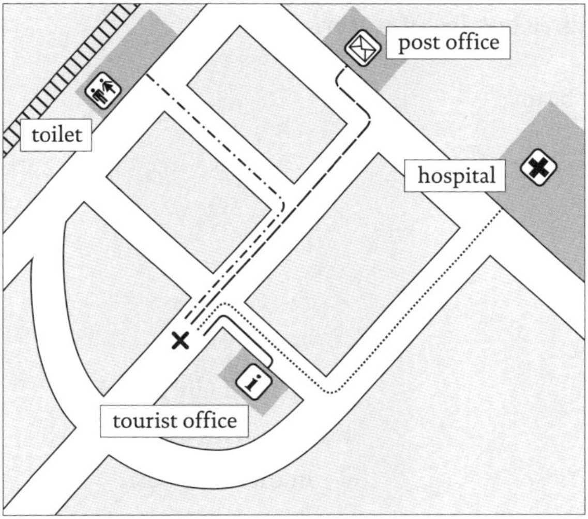

2 2 Minuten,

group	dark	flag	fight	drink	feed	look	thing
soup	**park**	**bag**	**light**	**think**	**read**	**book**	**bring**

3 2 Minuten,

My birthday will be **on** Friday.
Maybe I'll get some table tennis balls **from** my parents. I'm very good **at** table tennis. My friend Dominic often plays **with** me. I asked him: "What **about** a game of table tennis?" I'm waiting **for** him now. I've already put up the table **in** the garden.

4 2 Minuten,

- a What are you reading? I'm **reading** a book.
- b Who are you talking to? **I'm talking** to Mary.
- c What are Lisa and Tom drinking? **They're drinking** some tomato juice.
- d Why are you two laughing? **We're laughing** because the picture is so funny.

e Where is Ben playing football? **He's playing football** on the playground.

5 2 Minuten,

Mrs Warren bought three **bottles of water**,
a **box of** chocolates,
two packets of jelly beans,
a packet **of biscuits**,
a bottle of milk.

Klassenarbeit 4

1 7 Minuten,

1 Ella and Lily are
2 Ella wasn't
3 She was
4 Ella brought
5 Ella put
6 Mrs Silverstone is
7 Nobody else had
8 The pupils had played
9 Mrs Silverstone used

a Ella and Lily's teacher.
b a pet with them.
c in the same class.
d the hamster for a lesson.
e her hamster to school.
f an April fool's trick on Ella.
g at school on the last day of March.
h ill.
i the cage with the hamster on her table.

1	2	3	4	5	6	7	8	9
c	g	h	e	i	a	b	f	d

2 4 Minuten,

a Here we are **sitting** *(sit)* in front of our tent. It's a wonderful morning.
b The sun **is shining** *(shine)*.
c We **are having** *(have)* breakfast.
d Kristy, my wife, **is wearing** *(wear)* a big hat and sunglasses.
e Our children **are playing** *(play)* cards.
f Timmy, our dog, **is watching** *(watch)* them.

3 4 Minuten,

a What is Vincent eating?
b Where is Vincent sitting?
c Why is he sitting in the garden?
d Who is lying next to him?
e When is Vincent having lunch?

4 5 Minuten,

a There is **some** jam in the fridge.
b There is also **some** cheese in it.
c But there aren't **any** sausages in it.
d There **aren't any** apples.
e Is there **any** salad in the fridge? – **Yes, there is.**
f And there are **some** eggs in it.
g There is also **a banana and some butter (in the fridge).**

5 10 Minuten,

Patrick sagt, dass er ein Geschenk für seinen Vater kaufen möchte.
I would like to buy a present for my father.

Die Verkäuferin fragt, was er kaufen möchte.
What would you like to buy?

Patrick sagt, er weiß es nicht.
I don't know.

Die Verkäuferin fragt, ob sein Vater Bier mag.
Does your father like beer?

Patrick bejaht.
Yes, he does.

Die Verkäuferin fragt, ob ihm das Bierglas mit dem Big Ben darauf gefällt.
Do you like the beer glass with Big Ben on it?

Patrick sagt, dass es schön ist.
Yes, it's nice.

Patrick fragt nach dem Preis.
How much is it?

Die Verkäuferin sagt, dass es nicht teuer ist und nur 3,50 £ kostet.
It's not expensive. It's only £ 3.50.

Patrick sagt, dass er es nimmt.
I'll take it.

Patrick bittet die Verkäuferin, es in eine Schachtel zu tun.
Could you put it in a box?

Test 5

1 9 Minuten,

Hörverstehenstext (Track 7):

Holiday memories

The Hoons
We cycled along National Cycle Road, which follows Hadrian's Wall. Fortunately we had warm and sunny weather the whole day. The wall was started to be built in AD 122 during the rule of the Roman emperor Hadrian. It took about six years to finish the wall. It was 120 km long and a big part of the wall still exists today. It was built to protect the Roman Empire from the people that lived in northern Britannia.

The Todds
My husband is a football fan. Yes, he likes football very much. His favourite club is FC Chelsea. But when we were in Manchester last summer he wanted to see the stadiums of Manchester City and Manchester United. First he went to the Etihad Stadium, which is the stadium where Manchester City plays. It offers seats for 47 000 spectators. It was opened in 2002 by Queen Elizabeth. Originally it was built for athletics events, but it was changed to a football stadium in 2003.
Next day he took part in a tour around the Old Trafford. It's the home of Manchester United. The first stadium at this place was built in 1910, so it is much older than the Etihad Stadium and it is much larger with seats for 76 000 spectators.

The Macmillans
We spent our holiday in the Lake District. We climbed Skiddaw, which is a mountain about 931 m high. It's one of the highest mountains in the Lake District and is situated near Keswick. Lincoln Guest House, where we stayed for a week, is in Keswick, too. Keswick is a little town with about 5 000 inhabitants. There is a famous pencil museum. It shows the manufacturing history of pencils and how pencils have been used through the ages. They exhibit the world's longest colour pencil.

The Hillstones 17

In our last holiday we stayed in York. We were there for the second time in the same hotel. We had stayed there two years ago. We like that hotel very much. It's only an 8 minute-walk to the town centre and they have very good food. Right in the centre of York is the minster. It's one of the largest Gothic cathedrals in Northern Europe. This time we booked a tour around the minster. It was built between around 1220 and 1470. In 1984 a fire caused by a flash of lightning destroyed much of the roof. Restoration work took four years and cost 2.4 million pounds.

a

The Macmillans

The Hoons

The Hillstones

The Todds

b

	right	wrong
The weather was nice when the Hoons went along Hadrian's Wall.	✓	
Hadrian's Wall was built by the Romans.	✓	
Mr Todd is a football player.		✓
Old Trafford is the stadium of Manchester City.		✓
Manchester United's stadium is much bigger than Manchester City's stadium.	✓	
The Macmillans stayed in a big city in the Lake District.		✓
The Macmillans visited a pencil museum.	✓	
The Hillstones went to York for the first time.		✓
The Hillstones took part in a tour around the city of York.		✓

2 1 Minute,

Monte Rosa is a very high mountain in the Alps. It is the highest mountain in Switzerland. Mont Blanc is **the highest** mountain in France. Mont Blanc is **higher than** Monte Rosa. At 4 810 m it is **the highest** mountain in Europe.

3 3 Minuten,

One of the **most expensive** fish is the koi. You must keep koi in a little pond. An aquarium is too small for them. Some people think they are **the nicest** fish in the world. Other people think betta are even **nicer than** koi. But you must keep them alone in an aquarium because they are very aggressive. Guppies are **easier** to keep and quite popular. But goldfish are **more popular than** guppies. They are one of the **most popular** aquarium fish in the world.

4 2 Minuten,

b young / **old**
c expensive / **cheap**
d ugly / **beautiful** (**nice**)
e early / **late**
f difficult / **easy**
g sad / **happy**
h bad / **good**
i short / **long**
j slow / **fast** (**quick**)
k small / **tall** (**big**)

Klassenarbeit 5

1 10 Minuten,

a **Weil die Enten der Ratcliffs den Salat im Garten der Masons aufgefressen haben.**
b The Masons had **a small garden** behind their house.
c Their neighbours, the Ratcliffs, were **farmers**.
d Every year in May Mrs Mason **planted some vegetables**.
e One morning Ricky shouted: “The Ratcliffs’ ducks **are in our garden and are eating our salad!**”

f Mrs Ratcliff ran out but **it was too late**.
g The garden **was ruined**.
h The ducks had eaten **most of the plants**.
i Mrs Ratcliff felt **very sorry for Mrs Mason**.
j Some days before Christmas **Mrs Ratcliff took a parcel to Mrs Mason**.
k In the parcel there was **a fat duck** and **a piece of paper**.

2 1 Minute,

cheap	**cheaper**	*the cheapest*
popular	*more popular*	**the most popular**
early	*earlier*	**the earliest**
good	**better**	**the best**
bad	**worse**	**the worst**

3 5 Minuten,

a This is my father. He is 42 years old. He is **the oldest** in our family. I've got two sisters, Leah and Victoria. This is Leah; she is my **youngest** sister. She is **the smallest** in our family. Victoria plays the piano and the violin. She is **the most musical** member of our family. Can you see my brother Andrew? It is not difficult because he is **the tallest**. Can you find me? I always buy **the most beautiful** and **most modern** clothes I can find in the shops. And there is our mother. I think she is **the busiest**, **the nicest** and **the most intelligent** woman in the world. We all love her.

b 1 **father/dad** 2 **mother/mum** 3 **Leah**
4 **Victoria** 5 **me** 6 **Andrew**

4 2 Minuten,

a Allan's father **couldn't smoke** cigarettes.
b Allan **could take** photos of the wax models.
c They **couldn't take** their dog with them.
d They **could buy** some souvenirs.
e They **couldn't touch** the wax models.

5 5 Minuten,

a Did you like London? Yes, I really liked it there.
b How long **did** you **stay** in London? I stayed in London for five days.
c **Did you go** with your family? – Yes, I did. I went with my parents and my brother.
d **Did you stay** at a hotel? – No, we didn't. We stayed at a friend's house.
e Was it your first time in London? – No, it **wasn't**.
f **Did you see the Queen?** No, we didn't see the Queen.
g Did you see "The Shard", the highest building in London? – Yes, we **did**.
h Did you go on a boat tour on the River Thames? – No, we **didn't**.
i **Did** your parents and your brother like London, too? Yes, **they did**.

6 7 Minuten,

a Our last trip to Ireland was very nice.
b I would like to go to Ireland next year, too.
c I would go on holiday with my parents if they don't go to Ireland.
d I don't want to go away this year.
e What will you do then?
f I will stay at home. I will save for a new bike.
g We can talk about it.

Test 6

1 8 Minuten,

Hörverstehenstext (Track 8):

Mr Cain: Good morning, Mrs Moore. You got up early today.

Mrs Moore: Hello Mr Cain. Yes, well I wanted to do some shopping before it rains again. What do you think about this weather? Terrible, isn't it?

Mr Cain: You're right. It's awful: rain, rain and more rain.

Mrs Moore: Yes, I'm really fed up with this weather. I don't think we've seen any sunshine for about three weeks.

Mr Cain: You're right. Three weeks at least.

Mrs Moore: I said to my husband, "Let's go to Spain for our holiday this year. Maybe we'll get some sunshine there." And we booked yesterday.

Mr Cain: That's a good idea. When are you going?

Mrs Moore: In a month, on 5th July.

Mr Cain: And for how long?

Mrs Moore: For two weeks. By the way, could you water our flowers and feed our cat while we are away?

Mr Cain: On the 5th you said? I'm so sorry, but we're going on holiday to Italy on the 6th ourselves. But we can take you to the airport in our car, if you like.

Mrs Moore: That would be nice.

Mr Cain: But why don't you ask the Smiths next door? Their son is coming from Australia to visit them for a week at the beginning of July. So they won't be away.

Mrs Moore: Oh, that's good news. I'll go and ask them at once.

a Is Mrs Moore talking to Mr Cain <u>in the morning</u> or in the evening?
b Have they had fine weather or <u>bad weather</u> for a long time?
c Are they talking to each other in <u>June</u> or July?
d Are the Moores going to <u>Spain</u> or to Italy?
e Are the Cains going on holiday at exactly the same time as the Moores or <u>one day later</u>?
f Are the Moores going to Spain by car or <u>by plane</u>?
g Are the Moores going on holiday because <u>they don't like the weather at home</u> or because they want to visit their son?
h Do the Moores have a dog or <u>a cat</u>?
i Is the Smiths' son coming from <u>Australia</u> or from Austria?
j Will the Moores be away <u>for two weeks</u> or for three weeks?

2 5 Minuten,

a It's sunny.
b It will rain. / It will be rainy.
c No, it won't. (It will be foggy.)
d No, it isn't. (It's cloudy.)
e Yes, it will.
f Today it is rainy with a little bit of sun. Tomorrow it will be sunny.

3 2 Minuten,

a morning – evening – ~~clock~~ – afternoon – night
b ~~year~~ – autumn – spring – winter – summer

c carrot – chocolate – bread – cheeseburger – ~~cook~~
d longer – better – ~~driver~~ – higher – nicer
e cloudy – sunny – snowy – ~~busy~~ – rainy

Klassenarbeit 6

1 7 Minuten,

Hörverstehenstext (Track 9):

The old man and the tiger

On his way through town a policeman met an old man walking with a tiger on a leash.

POLICEMAN: What are you doing with that tiger here in the park?

MAN: Well, this morning I found him lying in front of my garden gate. He had a piece of glass in his front paw. He was bleeding very much. I pulled out the piece of glass and now I'm going for a walk with him.

POLICEMAN: I see, that's very nice of you, but you'd better take him to the zoo.

MAN: That's a good idea. I'll do that tomorrow.

The next day the policeman met the man again with the tiger on the leash near the cinema.

POLICEMAN: What are you doing here again with your tiger? Didn't I tell you to take that tiger to the zoo?

MAN: Sure you did, and he liked it very much there. But today I want to take him to the cinema. He liked the film on my television very much yesterday evening.

		right	wrong
a	A policeman met an old man on his way through town.	✓	
b	The man had a tiger on a leash *(Leine)*.	✓	
c	He had found the tiger in the park.		✓
d	The tiger had hurt one of its front paws.	✓	
e	The policeman told the old man to take the tiger to the doctor.		✓
f	The next day the policeman met the old man with the tiger again.	✓	
g	This time he wanted to watch TV with the tiger.		✓

2 10 Minuten,

a One ~~night~~ Robin Hood met a strange knight.
One morning Robin Hood met a strange knight.

b ~~Marian~~ jumped down from ~~her~~ horse.
Robin jumped down from his horse.

c ~~Marian~~ put a wet cloth on ~~Robin's~~ forehead.
Robin put a wet cloth on Marian's forehead.

d Marian gave Robin a letter from the ~~king~~.
Marian gave Robin a letter from the queen.

e It was an invitation to the ~~queen's picnic~~ on Saturday.
It was an invitation to the king's archery competition on Saturday.

f Robin will go there with ~~Maid Marian~~.
Robin will go there with his friends.

3 5 Minuten,

a	What **will you get?**	I think I'll get a CD.
b	Where **will you travel?**	We'll travel to Italy this year.
c	Will you go by plane?	No, **we won't**. We**'ll go** by car.
d	Will the weather be sunny tomorrow?	No, **it won't**. **It'll be** rainy.
e	When **will Manchester United play against Chelsea?**	Manchester United will play against Chelsea on Wednesday.
f	Where **will they play?**	They'll play in London.
g	Who will win?	I think Manchester **will win**.

4 8 Minuten,

Cedric:
He will be happy in love. He won't get more pocket money. His marks in maths will be OK.

Karen:
She won't go on holiday. She will get a present. She will have a new friend.

Benedict and Jane:
They will make an excursion. They will get a guitar. They won't go to school.

Test 7

1 6 Minuten,

Hörverstehenstext (Track 10):

My Halloween

Halloween is the night when children in the USA dress up as ghosts and witches.
On 31st October my friends and I always go from house to house to beg for candies. First we ring the doorbell. When the people open the door we say a little rhyme: "We jump over fences and ditches because we're ghosts, robbers and witches." Then we shout: "Trick or treat!" Most people give us a handful of candies or a bar of chocolate, some chewing gum or even a bottle of coke. This year an old man opened the door, listened to our rhyme and then shouted: "Go away! Buy your candies yourselves." So we had to play a trick on him. We went to his house several times that evening and rang his doorbell. But before he could open the door we ran away and laughed.

a On Halloween children in the USA dress up as ~~clowns~~ and witches.
On Halloween children in the USA dress up as ghosts and witches.

b On ~~30th~~ October they go from house to house.
On 31th October they go from house to house.

c They shout "Trick or ~~sweet~~!" and often get candies.
They shout "Trick or treat!" and often get candies.

d This year an old ~~woman~~ didn't give them anything.
This year an old man didn't give them anything.

e So the children played a trick on him; they rang the ~~phone~~ several times and ran away.
So the children played a trick on him; they rang the bell several times and ran away.

2 2 Minuten,

a Last year we went on holiday with **our** friends in **their** car.

b On the way the car made a strange noise. So they had to take **it** to a garage at once.

c Our friends wanted to buy some souvenirs. So we went shopping with **them**.
d Tim, their little son, likes building sandcastles. So they went to the beach with **him**.
e My sister wanted a new dress, but my parents didn't buy one for **her**.
f After a week we had to go home again. It was a nice holiday for all of **us**.

3 2 Minuten,

a aunt – mother – grandfather – daughter – cousin – **sister/brother/…**
b flat – castle – tent – cottage – **house/apartment/…**
c video recorder – digital camera – mobile phone – **TV/mp3-player/ …**
d run – go – drive – ride – **walk /…**
e car – caravan – train – taxi – **bus/coach/…**

4 5 Minuten,

Dear Peter,
Yesterday I got up too late. My mum didn't hear the alarm clock. I ran to the bus station, but I missed the bus. I won't get up so late tomorrow. Next week I'll go to school by bike.
See you, Tom

Klassenarbeit 7

1 8 Minuten,

a Es befindet sich in Montrose.
b Es ist sehr modern, es hat einen Garten und eine Garage.
c Es hat eine Küche, drei Schlafzimmer, ein Ess- und ein Wohnzimmer, eine Toilette und ein Badezimmer.
d Ja, es gibt einen Fernseher.
e Man kann ins Kino gehen.
f Die Städte Dundee und Aberdeen sind in der Nähe.
g Es ist nicht weit, nur 45 km und man kann mit dem Auto fahren oder mit dem Zug.
h Ja, können sie, aber sie dürfen auch das Auto der Smiths nehmen.

2 6 Minuten,

Mia was at the supermarket last Monday. She **wanted** to buy ice cream and **looked** for her favourite ice cream in the freezer. Suddenly she **saw** a mobile phone at the bottom of the freezer. "A mobile phone doesn't belong in a freezer", she **thought**. Somebody must have forgotten it. She **took** the mobile phone and **went** to the girl at the checkout *(Kasse)*.
"I **found** this mobile phone in the freezer. I think somebody left it there."
The girl at the checkout **said**: "Oh dear! It's my mobile phone! I've missed it the whole day. I must have forgotten it there this morning. Thanks a lot." Then she **said**: "Go back to the freezer and take the biggest box of ice cream you want. I'll pay for it."

3 5 Minuten,

Vincent often goes to see his grandparents in the country. They **have** a farm with a lot of animals. Vincent always **takes** the train at 11.15 to Hereford when he **visits** his grandparents at the weekend. The train **arrives** in Hereford at 12.30. His grandmother always **waits** for him at the station. Then they **go** to the farm by car.

Vincent is showing you some photos from the farm:

"In the left picture you can see grandma. She is picking plums.
In the other picture you can see my cousin Tina. She **is milking** a cow."

"This is me. **I'm feeding** the horse. In the other picture you can see my grandpa. He **is carrying** a lamb."

4 5 Minuten,

								1 h										
			2 d	i	c	3 t	i	o	n	a	r	4 y						
						e		l				e					8 b	
						a		i				a					o	
		5 h		6 b				d			7 b	r	o	t	h	e	r	
	9 p	o	l	i	c	e	m	a	n								i	
		r		k				y									n	
		s		e				10 s	e	11 l	l						g	
		e								o								
										n								
							12 l	a	n	g	u	a	g	e	s			

5 3 Minuten,

- **a** Holly is going to see a film at the cinema.
- **b** Michael is going to go to the music store to listen to some CDs.
- **c** Sarah and Susan are going to play tennis.
- **d** Robby is going to do his homework.
- **e** Daniel and Brian are going to do nothing.
- **f** I am going to go to school.

6 8 Minuten,

Doris fragt Brian, was er letztes Wochenende gemacht hat.
What did you do last weekend?

Brian sagt, dass er mit seiner Familie campen war.
I was camping/at the campsite with my family.

Doris fragt, wo sie campen waren.
Where did you camp?

Brian sagt, dass sie am Loch Ness waren.
We were at Loch Ness.

Doris fragt, ob er Nessie gesehen hat.
Did you see Nessie?

Brian sagt, dass er Nessie nicht gesehen hat.
No, I didn't see Nessie.

Doris fragt, was er nächstes Wochenende macht.
What are you going to do next weekend?

Brian sagt, dass sie sich treffen könnten.
We could meet.

Doris sagt, dass das toll wäre.
That would be great.

Lösungsheft zu Klassenarbeiten Englisch 6. Klasse
Hauptschule
Best.-Nr. 1035561